Two

Story by June Melser
Illustrations by Isabel Lowe

2

3

The two little dogs
ran after a cat.

They ran after a bird.

They ran after a mouse.

They ran after a rabbit.

"Look! A big, big dog."

"That's bad!" they said.

"We won't run after **him**."

And they didn't.

He ran after **them**

all the way home.

14

15